women in the waiting room

women in the waiting room

kirun kapur

Black
Lawrence
Press

www.blacklawrence.com

Executive Editor: Diane Goettel
Cover Design: Zoe Norvel
Cover Art: "I Am No. 2" by Elizabeth Becker
Book Design: Amy Freels

Copyright © 2020 Kirun Kapur
ISBN: 978-1-62557-823-5

Published 2020 by Black Lawrence Press.
Printed in the United States.

For all the voices,
all the echoes

&

for Jamie, without whom I couldn't find my own

Contents

On Looking at Myself in the Mirror, Or,
    Re-Reading Valmiki's Ramayana   3
Girls Girls Girls   5
Hotline   7
Steubenville Ghazal   9
The Annunciation   11
Hotline   13
In the Rub' al Khali   15
Sea Anemone   18
Hotline   20
Motorcycles   22
Hotline   23
Waiting for Sleep, I Imagine Sita in Her Youth   25

Women in the Waiting Room   29

Red Lilies Ghazal   47
By Wind is the Tree Cut Back   48
Pelvis with Distance (Georgia O'Keeffe, 1943)   50
Kyphosis   52
Treatment   54
Hotline   56
Sleeplessness, Or, Imagining Sita Preparing to
    Step into the Fire   58

Hotline   61
Uselessness Ghazal   63
The Bird Watchers   65
Spring   68
Hotline   69
Reincarnation Ghazal   71
Parvati at Her Bath   73
the one with violets in her lap   76
Let Me Be As a River   78

Notes   79
Acknowledgments   80

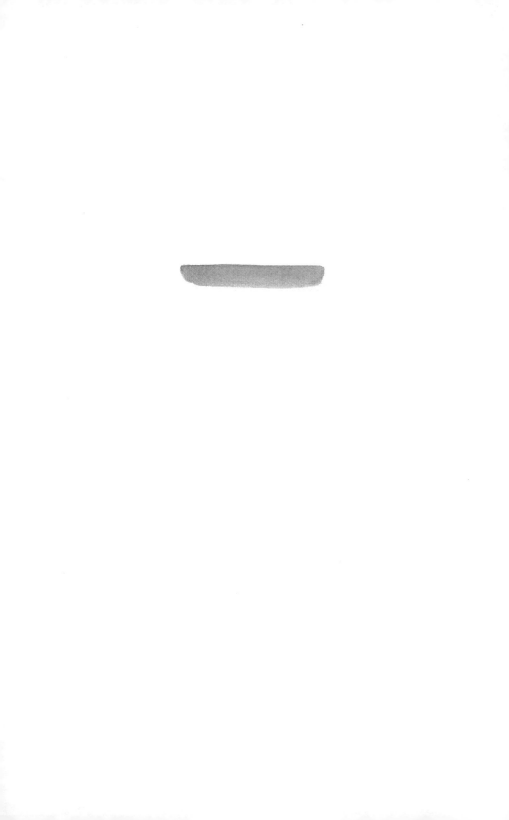

On Looking at Myself in the Mirror,
Or, Re-Reading Valmiki's Ramayana

Anyone can disappear
across the black water.

Every girl can be taught
her middle name is shame.

When will I burn
the urge for purity—

my bones are a furnace
my face is a game.

Every girl steals away
with a demon at some point—

all her alphabets, ankle bells
all her braids—

She will meet herself in the third person,
she will lie with her fear,

she will dress in her rage.

The world is curdled

with husbands,

blue as the gods, gentle as flame.

Girls Girls Girls

Along the strip in Waikiki, past sailor bars
and clubs, the length of beach where lipstick
sunsets smudged and magazines would shoot
and caption, *Paradise*. Past posh hotels
where M. and I would wait for some nice man
to buy us drinks from the bar. We'd watch
the women walk like they were stars onstage,
dress like they couldn't wait to be undressed,
leaning over into idling cars. Out on the west side
of the island, J. tells me any man she dates
is more likely to hit her than pay for her dinner.
Teenagers holding babies spit at us when we stare:
What you looking at? You got nothing.
I have nothing, sobs L., today, on the phone.
I know it isn't my fault, but when I think of how I let him do it
over and over, even helped him cover it up, I hate myself.
I'm thinking of the man who owned the noodle shop,
the man who'd always sit with me and chat
about Hanoi, warm water in canals,
moms on bikes with babies tied down
front and back, how to tell a ripe papaya.
I saw him on the news a few years back,
for smuggling women in refrigerated trucks.

He owned the bar called *Girls Girls Girls*

a few doors down from where he served me pho,

the one whose sign was made of neon legs

that kicked and kicked until they were a stain of light.

We liked to swim along the south shore

when the tide was right. You had to time your dive

or crack your head against the reef. More than once

a girl washed up. Sometimes they named her

on the news. M. and I drank Kamikazes

on the lanai of the new Sheraton,

the chief of security coming out to check

we were the right sort of girls, regaling us

with stories of the wallets stolen off businessmen

by *ladies* visiting their rooms, a theft

they'd later blame on the hotel maid.

I hate—L.'s voice, mine. *When I think*

of how I—how times have I said it?

How many times have I said nothing at all

or tried to explain why we aren't at home—

the right sort of girl and the wrong, why

we're out under the orange street lights.

Hotline

I have been trained
so when she says,   *I watched my father*
smash my mother's forehead with a wooden broom handle,
I show no sign of shock.

        The poet   liked to say, *you shouldn't*
        borrow sorrow.
        Write real things: dish pans, porch screens,
        broom handles. *Give me*
        a humble trash bag.

For years   this face
I trained my mind to un-see—
cheek eaten   away by fish,
girl-body, washed up
in the canal,   wrapped—
the brand identified as *Glad.*
No scars,   birthmarks,   clothes,   jewelry,

5'2, 133, precisely
my own height and weight.

                              Police   were saying
                              was she sure it was a broom handle?
                              Metal or wooden? We need
                              the details right. How could
                              a wooden handle   do all that?

The poet suggests,
make it a skillet. *I'd believe*
he killed her with a skillet,   if you must.

                              On the page,   I describe
                              lilies wilting in the vase,
                                        because I have been trained,
                              because you have been trained—
                                                  can you   believe
                              six glistening stamens,
                              smashed   rust-velvet anthers.

8

Steubenville Ghazal

Steubenville High School, Ohio, 2013

It was hard not to notice the style of him.
We were all mesmerized by the smile on him.

Snaps, sexts. He might. I might not.
Friends teased, *Post a pic of your thigh for him.*

There's a strip mall, a steel mill, the long Veterans Bridge.
The white picket grin was the lie of him.

A basement. The music. Coats draped on the couch.
I kept drinking and thinking, *Don't be shy with him.*

He posed for the camera, his hand on my neck.
I lay still underneath the hard guile of him.

I dream I'm clear wind, I dream I'm blank space,
I dream of the girl who's surviving him.

Skank. Slut. Cunt. Whore.
What did you expect? is the cry from them.

Skank. Slut. Cunt. Whore.

These are the facts from the trial of him.

In Delhi, a bus. In Houston, a bridge.

There's New Bedford, Toronto, Dubai for him.

For a girl to be innocent she has to be dead.

The newspapers await a reply from him.

My name is redacted, it no longer applies.

I end every line writing *him, him, him.*

The Annunciation

It will come down to he said, she said.

The color of sunlight and shade, what could be heard from the street,
whether the spider lilies were still blooming.

The great I AM spoken by one
swallowed, in silence, by the other.

Many times a day she will try to think of lying there
his shadow crossed over her, but will conjure nothing.

Other times she will wake with the feel of a tongue, wet in her ear
though she has sat for hours on the shower floor scrubbing her face away.

Behold—a word of witness.

So much went unrecorded between the girl and the Angel.

Did it pour down like honey? Did it sting?

The soul, whatever it is, struggles to articulate.

She can still go to that place, where nothing grows,

where her mind has nothing in it and only breath

ties her to the world with a blue hair ribbon.

The movement of the soul toward articulation is slow.

No official complaint has been recorded.

It is known that she was clutching a book,

that through the whole ordeal she kept one finger in the page.

Behold: a word of holding steady

in the mind, in the eye.

Later, they will ask why didn't she drop it, use it to push him away.

No, it was not the first time she'd been in his garden.

Yes, willingly, she may have claimed to be his.

It felt good to be held, until she felt nothing.

Hotline

She said, *I did have a lot to drink*

           She said, *I did say he could come in*

     It was fall   *I could smell the leaves*

      I could see the ghost of my breath

      He kept saying   *he*

loved me

         It's a relief   *such a relief*

Sometimes I do it while I pray

              She said, *I hope it's ok that I'm calling*

I need to hear a human voice today   She said,   *Do you think it's a sin*

Do you think God won't save me if he knows

I love to cut my skin

Is it ok for me to say that here?

She said, *I'm not*   *harming myself*

I'm making myself feel free

I've read that nuns were allowed to
starve

themselves

It was holy,   *then*

In the Rub' al Khali

I.

You'll want to cover yourself. The morning
cry from the Muezzin strips the sky.

Ptolemy was first to reveal
the desert's entry gate to the world,

calling Muscat, *hidden harbor*. You believe
all any person wants is to be seen,

but here you stand under the cloudless eye
and know how Eve and Adam felt—

sweet and tart fruit lashed their mouth
transforming them: bare to exposed.

Wrap up your frankincense, your bridal chest
of meteor stones in layer after layer

of earthly cloth. When the day has glazed
you in its kiln, when you're the only

vertical line crossing the horizon,
it's a relief to kneel, drench your face

in fine red sand. Let's feed each other
a bowl of dates, let's build a courtyard garden

surrounded by high walls. Before the first prayer
ends and dawn blinds us with its charge,

let's trap the darkness, Love,
hold all its stars under our shawls.

2.

If satellites patrol our heaven,
if beetles leave encrypted tracks

around our sleeping mats
for a thousand mornings,

if our story orbits back
to when the desert was

the ocean, if
you put your mouth

to me like a jellyfish,
like a diesel kiss, like I am

a bottle of well water,
if we crush each other,

like a reef whose happy ending is
to be reborn as dunes. Beloved

caravan, sweet eon, wind erosion—
If it hasn't rained in years, we'll live

on miraculous green shoots,
as when our vows were new.

Sea Anemone

All mouth. This
has always been my problem—

body named for an earthy flower,
foot rooted in a coral bed.

Look below the surface, anyone
can see how fear began to live

with me—a hundred fish turning
suddenly, as though a single silver flank

had heaved. This is what happens
when touch stings. I spend nights

holding fury and spit. Somewhere above
air is free, there's the pull of moon's gold

lip, there's a smirk that grows
until it swallows the whole bed.

I wish I could accept
what's swept through me—

a rush of cooler water

stirred by rays, dust sloughed

from a shark's fin. I wasn't made to walk

away. I am the creature that stands

and sings into the miles of water—

Hear my raw throat,

salt tongue, my heartless bell.

Hotline

I was in the elevator it was　　　　　*the buckle on his belt*

I felt　　　*air got cold got*　　*stopped*　　　*feeling*

I couldn't enter this room I've entered hundreds of times before

　　　　one me lives there

　　　　　　　　　　in that room still

　　　　　　the other　　　*me*

　　just peeks in　　　　　　*just   occasionally*

　　　old me is dead

　Can you tell　　　　　*you're talking to a*

the problem is　　　*I couldn't save myself can't*

save can't change the problem　　　*is*

　　I wish the old me would　　　*just*

I went dancing last night

My father liked to say: I can tell   *you*   *what your problem is—*

      I was dancing and I could   *feel*   *her*

                            really   *I don't know*

if it felt   *good*   *feeling*

    her

        lifting her head

Motorcycles

Bare chrome, fast grin, hot pipes
Remind me I have skin. Piss off,

You plush backseats, I am a flag
Whipped taut in wind,

A cyclops with a golden eye—
I have a rampage caught between my knees.

When black road opens its throat,
When the engine kicks and kisses,

When I'm nothing but an articulate machine—
Drag bars, shaft drive, V twin. Darling,

If I idle like a tidal wave outside your door,
Come out, unwind me from my leather.

Hotline

She said,   *Don't make me tell you the story.*

        Don't   you   make   me—

that's something he used to say.

                              Three white undershirts

envelopes sticking to the floor by the front door

                    that's what she can remember.

I need someone alive who loves me

                              so with the last of her paycheck, she

            buys

tins of her cat's favorite food.

            She says,   *When I talk to myself*

                    I try to talk to myself like you   would

            talk to me.

She says,

                    Promise I won't always feel this way.

She leaves the T.V. on because she likes the voices

reminding her what to do:

Save all weekend at Eddy's—Get your news update—stay with us—
stay tuned—don't wait

Waiting for Sleep, I Imagine Sita in Her Youth

She hid all day in a tree,
ate guavas rubbed with salt and pepper,

stalked the long-haired cat, begged
for rotis, ghee and sugar,

watched as her mother dressed,
bangles stacking her arms like gauntlets.

From the window she could see
women from every corner of the city

walk into the river, disappear
then rise clean, saris soaking.

She drank milk from a hammered brass cup,
around her aunts, cousins unrolled their sleeping mats.

Of course a woman oiled her hair.
Of course a woman lined her eyes.

The inner world was made of women,
they filled her stomach, mouth, breath.

What do I need to see embroidered
in my mind's own dark? This girl

young enough to fall asleep. This dream
taking her into its current

so we might both rise ready
to wring out the story.

Women in the Waiting Room

Women in the waiting room wear turquoise
headscarves, jade shawls, lemon-yellow tees,
ongoing, their commitment to the flourishing world.
The hair goes. The breasts go. The ovaries. Gone
the uterus and fallopian tubes. This is the waiting room
of philosophers straightening lilac wraps, discerning
where the self resides without nipples or brows or two arms
likely to be the same width. Once, I was caught
shoplifting teal eye shadow. Waiting at the station for my father,
I was told that in some countries my hand would be cut off
for what I'd done. There was no imagining—blind shock,
blind ache, but I understood the shame of being punished
that way, as if my pride depended on remaining whole.
My father was so angry he didn't speak for weeks,
and so I learned the part of me that can't survive
without his voice. You, my friend, who have loved me
when I couldn't do that work myself, are being wheeled away.
I cling to your hand, then the bedrail, and then stand
in the fluorescent hall, while in your light blue gown, you go.

Sent up to bed some hours before, we'd traveled far

with flashlights under tented sheets, the stucco ceiling

standing in for stars. You were busy with my third grade

curls, my quarrelsome ends, while I described tall minarets

and crenelated walls, a white-washed compound

fringed with palms, the camel boys and how

a saddle slides as we climb a dune, then passed

the story off to you, taking the brush you handed me.

Your hair, already smooth as bolts of silk we carried

in our camel's pack, grew smoother still under my hands,

your sentence carting us to the walls of a desert city—

There was a sound downstairs, a grownup sound, somewhere,

outside, I could hear the revving engine of a car. We lay still,

a moment, inside our tent. Today, your hair feels just the same,

though short, your chemo-length. I make the nurses leave

your curtains closed, feed you ice, a luxury in desert places.

I trail a bald parade of ladies

through the maze of elevators, hallways,

seven-story building labeled *Parking Only*,

hatchback, minivan backed down a driveway

in the early hours, drove cold streets

or highways, minutes and hours and more,

to end here, neatly in a stall. The mind

rewinds—the keys, the parking pass,

the kind attendant stamping time, can't find

a sequence to the day: *Good news,*

the Patient Coordinator tells a woman

on the phone, *I can schedule the biopsy*

and surgical consult back-to-back.

I sit in garage twilight, in the stiff

front seat, feel mid-day light

pour through glass windows,

see nurses laughing in the corridors

rearrange their faces in a flash.

In the darkness of the post-op cubicle,

the world is once again a pulsing liquid place,

the womb, that first waiting room,

it seems reasonable to think about the soul.

What are its limits? What is it made of?

The IV drips, a nurse squeaks by in hot-pink shoes.

Here, the body seems to rule, and yet

you fix your voice, speaking to your daughter

on the phone, you tell your mother half the truth.

Inside you is a mass of will, still growing.

What are its limits? Of what is it made?

Soon, the surgeons will arrive with news.

Oncology, radiology, gynecology, epistemology,
malignancy, metastases, Ecclesiastes, genetic disease,
remission, superstition, permission, fatalism,
second opinion, mass, stained glass.

In order to debone a twelve-inch trout
your mother used two subtle movements
of the wrist, a flash of lacquer chopsticks,
then, from their tips the intact skeleton
hung graciously. A pot of broth was set
to boil. Rice noodles, translucent tongues
of meat arranged among jade vegetables.
I'm eight and twelve and seventeen. I've lost
a mushroom or a sliver of imported beef,
though I try to dredge the pot, repeatedly.
When your news first comes, the question
is *why*, a cry soon overcome by *how*, then
how long—time, the slow gold boiling
in your mother's pot. I watch you eating
mushroom soup a mile from where they
opened you. This rented room,
the mugs all chipped. We've measured
carefully, recorded fluid and blood
draining from your wounds. Your hands
maneuver steadily as though you move
chrysanthemum leaves on an antique plate.

Four can mean death, in Japanese.
When your mother speaks to me
I understand only every fifth word,
but we both pretend. Basho says,
spring passes, birds cry and the eyes
of fish are full of tears. When I describe
the doctor or the surgical margins
or what you're taking for the pain,
I can't be sure of what I've said.
She tells me I've caught the meaning
perfectly, a spring bird, a passing fish.

Side by side, in the motel's twin beds,
the room dark, the air conditioner clicking on
and off, we float words up into the wallpapered gloom,
we re-enact the nights when we were small,
the world a massive, ticking, unknown—lost time
alive again. Back and forth we pass the faces
of fourth-grade girls, the new infusion staff,
locations where we fought or danced or kissed
someone we'd just as soon forget. Neither of us speaks
about that night. For years I kept the shirt
you wrapped me in, buried my face
in the plain white quiet you laid over me.
When to speak and when to leave an empty space?
Today I had to pull your underwear back up.
Tonight, you're listing everything you'll never do—
have sex with the lights on, wear your purple strapless dress,
stand in the temple, year after year, saying prayers
for your mother's spirit. The future, the time
that might not be, is clear, here, in the dark
and I'm waiting for the moment when it's right
to make it stop, to interrupt.

Sporting three surgical drains, you text me
from a holiday performance, watching your girl
in a line with other girls. How many
will reach twenty with their mothers still alive,
how many will reach fifteen, ten, without
ever having wondered this? How many
will be tall or fast or good at chemistry?
How many. Thirty snowflakes shuffle
onto stage, execute their practiced twirl.

the night   the palm trees

                      sound like rain

    I

            voices   floors below

     you   in the street

in the head   it's time   what if I

         I   not

        no   I

            time it's time

You call to say you've found a small, new lump

beneath your ear. It's 2am, the dark so dark

I can't make out which room I've woken in,

the way it was when my son was new—

his cry, my staggering, while space bowed out

around us, cold volumes of a planetarium.

Tonight, the silence grows until we break

its shape with words: *fat deposit, swollen gland,*

likely to be nothing. Then plan for surgeries,

new meds, a battery of scans. All calls in the night

are calls to live under the unsolvable dome.

I reposition the phone. We go on exchanging sounds.

I count your breaths, as I do my son's.

The week. The weeks. The year.
The twelfth floor follows
the fifth. Honey. Hon. My Dear.
Are you the patient's family?
On a scale from one to ten,
how is the shooting/intermittent
rain that can't be seen from the CAT scan
waiting room? How is
the tingling, numbness
that blanks my brain?
Fuck you, I want to say,
to the beautiful young man looking
for your good vein.

Still, there are some things I can't say
in a body that's been opened and reopened,
dressed and undressed by strangers.
The cell we are locked in grows.
The breast that grew, undressed,
that is removed, and yet some part of us
continues forward, the opposite
of still, living on in the body's
dismemberment. We have tried so hard
to be clear with our words, we have tried
to love these bodies. *Be still,* a man told me.
Hold still, the radiation tech now says.
I lay under the body of silence, alive. You,
your chest unzipped, prepare to leap away.

When wind ruffles the short wisps of your hair

When your body becomes a dial turning toward the sun

When out of your mouth, a parade of soldiers carting guns

Oh matter, Oh creaturely nature

When you dream of pressing mouths to your breastlessness

When you drag a noose of hope and plastic tubing

When you know, exactly, what matters

When you know knowing doesn't matter at all

The river can carry a woman-sized tree trunk,

absorb the whole hillside's slurry. All the same,

I find a long stick in the reeds, clear a place

around the rocks where the geese patrol.

On the days when I am half a continent away,

when the surgeon is not yet awake, not thinking

of who will lie under the lights, I make coffee,

say your name, standing in my dark kitchen,

I say it. On the days when you call, finding a way

to describe holding a bouquet of your own hair,

the toxic ice-creep in your veins, I watch the last

whip of light blurring the far bank slip away.

It will be back tomorrow. I know better than to say so.

I make plans to go out and rake the dropped leaves,

send you an envelope full of rust and gold.

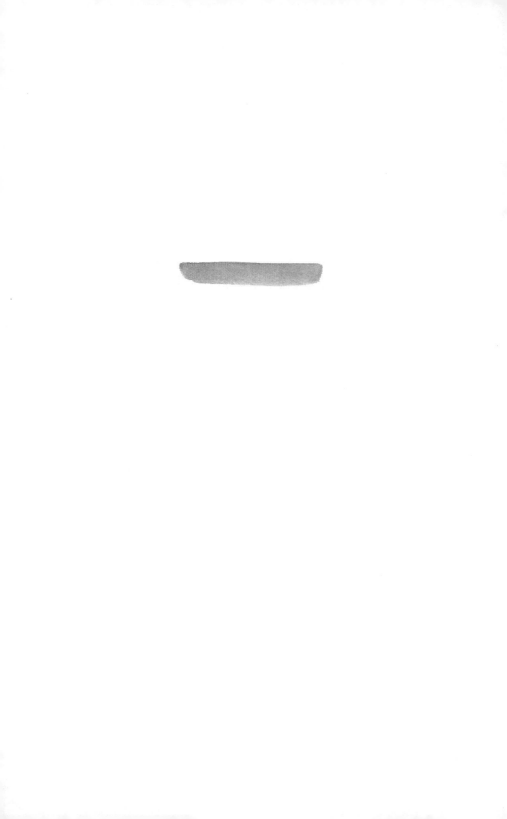

Red Lilies Ghazal

A chain of crushed nouns has upended my mind.
It's o.k. It's all right, pretended my mind.

A quick cut. A small nick. A surgical touch.
O Pethidine, Tramadol, so splendid my mind!

Ram drew back the string of King Janak's great bow,
Sita shot through the lifetimes and tended my mind.

Monkeys and blossoms, a long metal spine.
In the void, Frida's paintings befriended my mind.

Five parrots dive-bombing the pilkhan tree,
a sharp song, a green wingspan extended my mind.

The boat swamped with water, she lost hold of his hand.
Now she waits for a country that's abandoned its mind.

Red lilies lie drowned in a blizzard of snow.
Dear World, your bright terms have offended my mind.

What I? Which She? Who's writing this self?
A girl, years of girls, have escaped from my mind.

By Wind is the Tree Cut Back

and the upright animal
of me falls away

the knobs of my spine
stutter.

I broke a little bone
a vertebra—

a breath   a breath—
grasp every kind of chain.

No need for the whole
body, not in this place—

a room of wind,
a storm of doors—

pain is the strangest game.
I saw a woman on the floor

struggling to make a shape—

the body and the talk of the body
and in between long miles of white.

I broke my back.
No, says the brain.

The tree's trunk hacked
in half.

The woman will get up again

or in the blank—
the gasp—

she might stay.

Pelvis with Distance

(Georgia O'Keeffe, 1943)

Bone   and sky:
I waited my whole life

to be naked. Not nude,
which means unclothed

for the educated,
self-deluding eye—

that's not naked,
that was putting on clothes

of the character I played
to stir the camera's sighs

(a boy's hips, a boat's ribs,
breasts   like apricots,

a coarse curtain of hair
to pull or hide behind)

while critics lisped and gasped
about purity of line.

I   mean marrowed
by shrill trains of wind,

rilled by sunlight,
offered with no other

audience in mind.
Naked to myself, naked

to the God of all this space.
I mean bone and   sky.

Kyphosis

The god Hephaestus had it, too.
A yoke. A plow. A word

for punishment in public:
pillory. From *Kyphon,*

meaning bent or crooked.
I greet the diagnosis

with a recognition that's bone
deep. What twisted me,

what cause has hurt so long,
I hunch and barely notice it at all?

The surgeon's neat hands
demonstrate deformed

and fractured vertebrae.
His explanation's clean

and straight. He's not inclined
to metaphor. To work

under a weight— to show
your nature in your shape:

an ox, a crippled welder
of helmets and shields.

The lame one, the halting one,
maker of objects that can speak

to what's unfixable, hunch-backed
above the mouth of the forge.

Treatment

On the dark stage, the actress playing the young Sontag writhes
with books and longings. Oh Susan! The seriousness

with which she took her own mind and her ideas of pleasure—
Who has that kind of faith in themselves? Listen,

a finch is singing in the lilac. I can see the yellow body
in the leaves, its frantic chest, its shaking. I saw a girl once,

half-covered with burns—it was the doctor who saved her.
I must work, Sontag says, *That is everything and nothing.*

Deep into writing a book, she has her son take the cigarette
from her mouth, tap the long ash into a dish and place it back

in her lips, so that her typing wouldn't be delayed.
Five children had made it out of a fire,

three of them the doctors didn't take the time to treat.
Their mothers put their faces close

to whichever part looked least hurt. They talked.

One mother hummed a little song. To keep the heart beating,

the surgeon put a graft on the burned girl's chest.

On the stage, the cigarette smoke rises. Susan tries

to apply words to the surface of things. A badge. A skin.

It's not the same. But when nothing will ever be the same,

you find a treatment. More birds, more anesthetic, more

songs, more debridement.

Someday, you'll write about it, the surgeon later said.

The operating theater was empty. He was on his third drink,

I was still shaking. *No,* I answered. *Never.*

You will, he said. *I'm a doctor. Trust me.*

Hotline

If what

        he did to me has made me   *who I am*

        must I love him   *as I love me*   *I will cut off my own*

                    before I love the arms that—

    If—

      Can a person be made   *of a thing like that?*

Orioles are back.

           May I sing you a song

       I just called to sing a little song I wrote it's small—

       Where can I put it?   *It sounds like—*   *I want*

    to

put it down put everything away can a person   *like me be made—*

                 Hello? Hello?

Exactly

                                       what am I allowed to say?

          If

you can't   *repeat*   *what I say—he'll never know.*

How will anyone know what happened?   *To me.*   *Tonight*
If
       I can't even breathe.
                 Wait, this is confidential, right?
       ˒

                         Will you count with me?
So many little black birds with yellow wings did you

                know—
                      It's a just a short little
            song

      One

two   *three.*

Sleeplessness,
Or, Imagining Sita Preparing to Step into the Fire

In ticking minutes

                        I'm thinking

          I have slept beside one man

                         the shadows of others forcing me

     to the edge of the bed

                thinking

                          rose oil on her

breast,   bare orange

               blossoms wilted in bowls

        the night before the fire, how could she sleep

                             beside him

That air she breathes,

               damp like her face.

        All over him, holy

                        sandalwood paste.

I recognize her dream, just   before the world wakes,

                    to punish   what is loved

with righteousness.

        The demon had ten heads the demon had ten

                                    tongues—

One was enough,

surely.
One thing the demon gave her: freedom to hate

                the beloved's shape,

        clear in the low line of lamps,

                            the beloved's voice, carried

                    like a pot of water on a woman's head.

        In the forest   the story goes

                    she was   tricked   by a demon

appearing as a golden doe.   The story

        goes   when she stepped on to the pyre

                                        the fire could not touch her

because she was so pure.

                I'm tricked   again and again

                        by my urge to be good.

I'm waiting   for ten tongues

                        of light to appear on the ceiling,

        telling it all over again. I'm thinking of the washed rock

                        of her morning.   Telling

could change   the story,   couldn't it?

Hotline

My heart is a phone that's stopped ringing

        Don't confuse

                speaker and listener

                            counselor

        and caller

a sky of satellites that pass as stars

                            Have some faith

                            calls do go through

        Don't try to find the thread of sense

I lay completely still while   *one of them I loved*

                            for most of my life

Then my heart was still noisy

        It said What? What? What? What?

                            And the blood

        rushing

                                                        away from it

SHHH SHHH SHHHH

Now I'm telling you

        there's a neon crocus in the lawn

            Stop saying

            I don't think someone like you would speak that way

        If you can hear me   *you are the counselor*

if you're making these words   *in your mind*

        you're the caller too

Uselessness Ghazal

I've come down to face the river, Heraclitus.
Can't stop thinking, can't stop pacing, Heraclitus—

She said, *It happened 30 years ago, but it feels like yesterday.*
Some streams you can't step out of, Heraclitus.

The Great Grey Heron's legs look too long as she flies.
I feel the kinship of the wrongly-made, Heraclitus.

She said, *I should be over it. Beyond it. I should rise above.*
Would you claim suffering is prepositional, Heraclitus?

At the center of your town, a temple praising virgin Artemis.
May we be blessed by the many-breasted Lady of Ephesus, Heraclitus.

A body of water. A body of knowledge. A body of evidence. Body of crime.
You're called the weeping philosopher, Heraclitus.

She says, *It's like it happened to a different person, and yet...*
The drowned "I" can resurface with the tide, Heraclitus.

I listen. I pace. I say a helpless thing or two.

It's easier to argue terms with you, Heraclitus.

Change and time, these were your constant thoughts.

Centuries on, these are my useless comrades, too, Heraclitus.

The Bird Watchers

As if I'd stripped at a wake,
        when I came around the elderberry

humming this morning, I drew
        outraged stares, hisses

from the flock of ladies waiting
        in the blind for the Rough Winged Swallow.

Reminding me of the time I mistyped
        "prostate" for "prostrate," describing

funeral practices of Tibetan monks.
        It had been a rough-winged day—

out of jelly, a blouse with salad dressing
        stains, a small maestro who burped

the alphabet all the way to school.
        I'll confess, caught in their crosshairs

I didn't think of an apology, but of causing
        a flurry

of life-lists and sensible folding hats,
        annoyed by their silent rubber shoes.

On the drive to the wildlife sanctuary,
        a voice on the radio described how aerial

maps are drawn, lists and charts
        of where our bombs are meant to drop.

I parked my car between the painted lines.
        I double knotted my shoes.

What can a human animal do,
        but worship plumage? Who

wouldn't want to come up out of the dark water,
        as Mark says, and see the Spirit

descending like a dove? We've reached
        a standoff. Have I disrupted

their avian meditation or they my trudging
        prayer? So often fear and anger

feel the same these days, watching
        my own flutter as through binoculars.

Watch from the Old English

    Wacian: to be awake, to be watchful.

When my grandmother couldn't

    hold it steady anymore, I did

her lipstick for her. *I'm sorry*, we both said,

    when *Forever Red* feathered

her paper cheek. Next, I'll watch

    my mother-in-law go. Monk, dove,

there's always more humility

    to take. Should I beg

them to teach me tarsus, albumen,

    applause of wings, so I can sit beside

someone, my eyes on the long legs

    of the Snowy Egret, the shy

Brown Bittern, a furious little

    Kinglet defending her open space.

Spring

Then, through the window,
I could just make out a cormorant
immobile on a buoy, head high,
wings fully open, a totem,
black mark against morning.
I was about to turn away when it shifted,
twisting, slipping into the water,
first otter, then eel—a moment later
I could have sworn a girl with dark hair
surfaced. No time to blink
and the bird was back, swallowing prey,
lifting its head, pressing wings to the sun.
I watched to be sure it was real, a bird
who can escape—change shape after shape—
who can become a girl eating a river.
I've been two selves, at least,
two creatures, each hungry, each trying
to slip away. Bad-luck bird, snake,
girl—Can the sun burn from my chest
what chases me?

Hotline

When she asks,   *Are you a survivor, too?*

I do not say

I have been trained   not to answer that

On the page   I have learned: confession

is another mask

When she asks,

What do you do when you can't sleep? I don't explain

how I walk around

my small town

in the middle of the night to remind myself

I say,   *We're safe*

We count our breaths together

I hold on while she goes to get an ice-cube

goes to the bathroom, cries, murmurs, maybe

even sleeps

Are you still there?   She asks,   *Are you there?*

the self calling the self   back

        the poem I was trying to make

I'm here.   *I'm here.*   We take turns saying

Reincarnation Ghazal

I have looked back to see   my own body,

    unsure if it could really be my own   body.

The soft wood of the willow tree   splits easily—
    Who has the right to oversee   my body?

On TV, men smile,   white,   in fresh blue suits.

    I fill the doctor's forms regarding   my own body.

I count my breaths,   careful   slow,

    Friend, refuse   to be a refugee   from your body.

Laxmi was reborn as Sita; Mary carried   God as man.

    Did they ever want to flee   their human body?

Good years,   more years   I've watched her thinning skin—

    the woman who gave me   my own body.

Fixed high on the temple wall,   carved stone couples   twist.

Tourists wonder: *is that joy*   *a possibility*   *for my own body?*

The tulip   lost its petals   in the spring's warm wind.

What force   can set me free   in my own body?

Parvati at Her Bath

Once, I arrived to find Ana Christensen's mother
alone in the kitchen, eating chicken hearts.

And when Shiva arrived to find a strange child
guarding Parvati's bath, he cut off the boy's head

so that he could pass. And today, in bed 7a, is my soldier-friend
with a young god's face, his thighs pared down to flippers.

I've never seen anything like it, not even in a movie:
Mrs. Christensen's white-blonde head, her swan-blonde neck,

her cigarette unfurling as it rested on a bloodied plate.
The only sound was the clink of her knife and fork.

When Shiva left Parvati, he could disappear for an Age.
The goddess roamed the palace, trailing wind and her braid.

She ended the loneliness using turmeric and her own breath.
It was a boy she made, Ganesh, a son. His small heart

beating golden blood. Then, Shiva cut off the boy's head,
then Parvati stepped from the bath, then the whole

universe was nearly swallowed by a mother's rage.
My soldier and I play a game of where to rest

our eyes. *I want to die*, he tells me. *I think I've always
wanted to die*, and my mouth is filled with the taste:

blood-dirt, metal, chicken hearts and aquavit.
In a parking lot, I'd seen Ana Christensen's father,

his arm around the waist of some other woman.
What was Ganesh thinking not to step aside

when Shiva threatened? Why didn't he protest,
I'm the Goddess Parvati's son? Was he filled with fury

when Shiva gave him an elephant's head, made him
a beast, bringing him back to life? No one was surprised

when Ana Christensen's mother died of a failed liver.
Have you ever wanted to die, the legless god whispers?

It's spring again in this world. From the bank I watch
a whole dogwood tree, bobbing in the water.

The river can't hold everything that needs to be washed

downstream. I walk through what's left

at the edge: buoys, reeds, old lighters, a muskrat,

half its tail devoured.

the one with violets in her lap

after a line by Sappho

flower that can hardly whisper:

the prettiest thing about a girl

is her silence. A line broken

centuries ago. Scrap

of verse. of girl. Such loveliness

broken again, in time. Imagine

a corsage, a cloche, a petal pinned

to her shoulder under the chandelier—

Imagine an empty garden.

Dirt and silence

are what it takes to grow

a girl so quiet she can be written

down alive—a vase of

what happened

to *the one with violets in her lap*?

What survives survives

as fragment.

Let Me Be As a River

nothing but motion, muck
mouthed, mud hearted, brackish,
all dirty at the lip, with rise and fall
that exposes hull-gouging stones, no
curiosity about source, no knowledge
of destination, just willingness
to bear anything right to the end,
silver as fish skin, one hour
wrinkled, two hours smooth,
duck-fouled, trash-choked, silent
then gossiping under a full, red moon;
let me be dredged
when the leggy girls go missing,
used for a slow cruise, churned
for speed, reeking of the unseen
ocean or veiled in the scent
of pine trees, a fog in the head
then clear as the tip of a pin,
enough beauty to draw blood,
enough anger to strip the banks,
enough fullness to carry
the pleasure boats high.

Notes

1. The Steubenville rape case centered around members of the Steubenville high school football team who were accused of undressing, transporting, photographing, and repeatedly sexually assaulting a classmate while she was unconscious. Photographs, video, and commentary about the assault were shared among the students via social media. Two students were convicted, receiving the minimal juvenile sentences.
2. The Rub' al Khali is the largest contiguous sand desert in the world.
3. "Women in the Waiting Room" is dedicated to Mio Patricia Osaki.
4. "Treatment" was partially inspired by the play *Sontag: Reborn* and by a variety of biographies and memoirs, including Sigrid Nunez's *Sempre Susan.*
5. The title "the one with violets in her lap" is taken from Anne Carson's *If Not, Winter, Fragments of Sappho.*

Acknowledgments

Grateful acknowledgement is made to the editors of the following publications where these poems first appeared, sometimes in different forms:

AGNI ONLINE: "Girls Girls Girls"

Alaska Quarterly Review: "Women in the Waiting Room," "Hotline (She said, *I did have a lot to drink*)"

BlackBird: "In the Rub' al Khali," "Sea Anemone," "Motorcycles," "The Bird Watchers"

Chicago Quarterly Review: "On Looking at Myself in the Mirror..." (as "On Re-reading Valmiki's Ramayana")

Ginger: "Hotline (My Heart Is A Phone)," "Sleeplessness, Or, Imagining Sita Preparing to Step into the Fire," "Uselessness Ghazal"

Mantis: "Waiting for Sleep, I Imagine Sita in Her Youth"

Mom Egg Review: "Spring"

MumberMag: "Hotline (I Have Been Trained)," "the one with violets in her lap"

Philadelphia Review of Books: "Steubenville Ghazal"

Ploughshares: "Red Lilies Ghazal"

Prairie Schooner: "Parvati at Her Bath," "Pelvis with Distance (Georgia O'Keeffe, 1943)," "Treatment"

Raleigh Review: "The Annunciation," "Reincarnation Ghazal" (as "Incarnation Ghazal")

Salamander: "Kyphosis"

The Rumpus: "Hotline (When She asks)"

WILDNESS (UK): "By Wind is the Tree Cut Back"

"Let Me Be As a River" received the Nazim Hikmet prize and appears in the *Hikmet Prize Anthology*. "Girls Girls Girls" won a Best of the Net Award and appears in the *Best of the Net Anthology*.

Many friends have made this book deeper and better. I'm grateful to them all, especially Sandra Beasley, Brian Burt, Amy Clark, Carrie Green, Jessica Jacobs, Jennifer Jean, Danielle Jones-Pruett, Mark Jones, Elizabeth Knapp, Carla Panciera, Mike Perrow, Beth Woodcome Platow, Lynne Potts, Glenn Stowell, Kate Westhaver, Leslie Williams and Scott Withiam. Special thanks to Diane Goettel and the wonderful Black Lawrence Press for giving this collection a home. For endless support and wisdom, I thank all my parents: Terri and Inder Kapur, Jim and Letty Cash. For being at the heart, on and off the page, I thank Rachel DeWoskin and Fred Speers. For decades and continents of conversation, I thank Mark Vanhoenacker. For being with me in every room, first to final, I thank Mio Osaki.

Last and always, my gratitude to James Richard Cash and Silas Arjuna Cash who are the reason, the light, the best ending to every day and story.

Kirun Kapur grew up between Honolulu and New Delhi and now lives north of Boston. She is a poet, teacher and translator. Her previous collection, *Visiting Indira Gandhi's Palmist* (Elixir Press, 2015), was the winner of the *Arts & Letters* Rumi Prize in Poetry and the Antivenom Poetry Award. *Women in the Waiting Room* was a finalist for the National Poetry Series. Her work has appeared in *AGNI, Poetry International, Prairie Schooner, Ploughshares* and many other journals. She has taught creative writing at Boston University and Brandeis University, and has been granted fellowships from The Fine Arts Work Center in Provincetown, Vermont Studio Center and MacDowell Colony. Kirun serves as Poetry Editor at *The Drum Literary Magazine* and currently teaches at Amherst College. To learn more, visit her at kirunkapur.com.